Holy Mother Carry Us

Madonna Bond of the Free Ones

Holy Mother Carry Us

Madonna Bond of the Free Ones

DR. ANN MARIE NIELSEN

tNS
the NAMELESS
SPEAKS
PUBLICATIONS

MOTHER
CARRY
US

Being Infinity From Inside

The Diamond Abode of

Mother Father God

MOTHER CARRY US

Home

As The Eternal Love

Mother God

Carried

As The Carrying

Free Ones

Selah

Holy Mother Carry Us: Madonna Bond of the Free Ones

Copyright © 2017 by Dr. Ann Marie Nielsen

All rights reserved. No part of this book may be reproduced or transmitted in any form without the express permission in writing from the publisher, except by a reviewer who may quote brief passages for review purposes.

SECOND EDITION 2017

ISBN-13: 978-0-9975228-2-2
ISBN-10: 0-9975228-2-8

Published by The Nameless Speaks Publications, Florida USA

Set in Tramuntana 1 Text Pro

Front and back covers, page borders and interior art by Dr. Ann Marie Nielsen

www.motherahavah.com

Available worldwide from Amazon and other
online and traditional book sellers.

Prelude: Carried in the Real ... 13

Mother Ahavah Holy Mother Carry Us Awakening Art ... 17

Holy Mother Carry Us ... 23

The Bond In Black Madonna ... 35

Mother Ahavah, Mother's Love Notes ... 51

Divine Mother Primal & Practical ... 73

Additional Books by Dr. Ann Marie Nielsen

Pearls of the Presence

Diamonds of the Holy Heart

Father Ahavah

www.motherahavah.com

Prelude
Carried in the Real

Dear Reader,

It is a joy to share this Holy Mother chronicle message with you.

This presents a heart warming and heart awakening treatise on *The Real*. . . .

Being Carried in *The Real*. . . .

The Real in two ways:

1. The Absolute Immensity of Eternal Love, of Original Creator Light, with no other Awareness of anything other than that.

2. The direct instant by instant arising experience, exclusive of nothing — welcoming, inclusive, candid facing of every nuance

MOTHER CARRY US

and feeling — while simultaneously awakening as the full spectrum of aliveness of the ineffable tenderness and holiness of being face to face, One Heart to One Heart with and as Mother Father God Presence, while moving through every life experience, as authentic honesty, and open hearted vulnerable love.

This book message engenders unification
of the Absolute Real and the Phenomenal-Relative Real

Holy Mother Love

In the space between this or that

The Eternal Love space between the two

That makes not two

We live there

As we face each arising moment, each arising feeling, each arising relationship, each arising cry of the global condition — facing it more deeply, sensitively, keenly, honestly, majestically, than ever before — then we excavate all the way to translucent . . . all the way to discriminating loving-kindness.

MOTHER
CARRY
US

And as we keep facing and facing, from that meek anointing, one holy instant, we meet God face to face, breath to breath, intimate love to intimate love . . . Love.

As a species, as journeyers of this earthen five physical sense experience — it is time to no longer use the transcendent to escape from the imminent. Spring board this experience to remember Home, Eternal Presence.

Garner-reverence transcendence to reveal the mystery, the symbolism, the mirrored message in the imminent.

In this way, rather than negate our sacred responsibility to one another, we sensitize and esteem it. We arise as the Supreme Sensitivity of our natural scintillating Light-as-Love.

In coming alive as the Eternal Heart in sacred rhythm, we unify all the spectrums of Divine Mother dimensions, essences, wisdoms, principles, tendernesses.

We see that in radical, gentle, elegant, wild, sacred union with Divine Mother, the Vessel, we feel and know the reality of Father God. The Original Light lives us, as we express creative beauty in each moment.

We see that this fragmentary, volatile, disappearing world offers a forum for mastery in compassion, in piercingly-gently-pure Awareness.

Our translucency reveals the blackness of the void as gleaming with diamonds of Love.

We then remember the Dimond Abode, our true Home in each instant, each moment of tangibly-powerfully embraced, and tenderly experienced life.

Warm Blessings From My Heart,

Dr. Ann Marie Nielsen
Mother Ahavah

MOTHER
CARRY
US

Mother Ahavah
Holy Mother Carry Us
Awakening Art

Abiding with Contemplative Awakening Art

Awakening Art moves us far beyond looking at interesting or pretty pictures.

Awakening Art moves us beyond the narrow confines of ego limitations. It opens the vast vistas within the infinite center of our being. Contemplative art offers an invitation: *feel Home, alive as Love, aware as and in resonance as the rhythms of Light, the beauty of harmony.*

The paintings in *Holy Mother Carry Us* did not land upon the canvas to please or placate anyone, or with a thought of an aim or an audience. They arose spontaneously from a heart of love, and love's devotion, brilliantly clear in Presence.

MOTHER
CARRY
US

The colors and formations cascade from open vulnerability — they alight from the state of being wherein there is no beginning and no end.

The contemplative art offers many gifts for you. Seeing and feeling beauty uplifts us ever closer to the feeling of the beauty of holiness, the breathtaking beauty of our Creator. *Awakening the remembrance of the earlier Light beauty cocoons us, as it elevates us; it gently protects-soothes us while it liberates us.*

The contemplative art offers you . . . beckons you . . . to rest in the immortal nectar of nurture that fortifies you. This soft abiding opens pathways of remembrance of our Eternal Home.

To remember the Eternal Love of our Original Home, is to remember our True Essence.

As you contemplate the Awakening Art, along with resting in the written messages, we welcome you to invoke a soft prayer: to directly feel God; to gently and profoundly feel Love; and to sacredly and happily know your unique bejeweled, diamond value.

This, like Dr. Nielsen's other books, is not a book of learning. These are not words or images to consume.

This is a holy prayer scroll of remembrance . . . of tangible felt experience . . . of awakening in heavens way, on earth.

MOTHER CARRY US

As you abide with these paintings, your observation offers a gift to these art forms and further animates their expression of uplifting others in our world.

The Genesis of Holy Mother Carry Us book Paintings
And Mother Ahavah the Art Gallery

Without formal art training, and with no thinking or planning, the book and art author and artist, Dr. Ann Marie Nielsen, emanates, swirls and twirls out these heart-warming and evocative contemplative art paintings.

The delicate immensity of Mother God Love, one with Father God Love, shimmers from her heart, through her hands, to the paper and canvas.

Each painting or drawing generally completes in four to eighteen minutes—on average about nine minutes.

Each thirty seconds to a minute a new layer emerges of forms, colors, and wisdom principles known in consciousness, coming alive on canvas.

It's as if the formless Eternal Love expresses as shapes and colors, forms and images, that spark in us, the remembrance of Home.

MOTHER
CARRY
US

The first sketches/paintings occurred spontaneously in the fall of 2016. Feeling an immensity of divine devotion, and worshipful prayer, Ahavah (Dr. Ann Marie Nielsen) felt an impulse to express on paper in art forms. She rummaged around and discovered a few pieces of chalk.

Then she dug out a few odd, six dollar pot-of-paint sets, that she had tucked away on a hall shelf for when children visited. Having no brushes, she painted with her hands, a style she often uses to this day. A few of these early creations, she drew or painted with eyes closed or with her non-dominant hand.

We welcome you to immerse in the innocence, beauty and holy joy of these art creations, reflective of *Home*.

Rest in the Holy Mother Carry Us art, the remembrance of the beauty of Home.

Holy Mother Carry Us

The Bond in Black Madonna

Mother's Love Notes

MOTHER
CARRY
US

We symbolically leave the womb

Not only of a human mother —

We are taught as humans

To leave the womb *of being carried*

MOTHER
CARRY
US

Holy Mother Carry Us

ONLY THE STILL-EN-WOMBED
LIVE AS THE INFINITY OF LOVE

Holy Mother

Come to Us

Carry Us

One with You

Home

Home

Shalom

Home

All

All

All

Of our suffering

Stems from feeling

Existentially, fundamentally separate

From Creator

From Origin

From Love

All

All

All

Of our feeling separate

Stems from one primordial

Misconception

MOTHER
CARRY
US

A subtle twist of a nanosecond

Of a thought

Of having left the womb

Of Intimate union

With Divine Mother

Holy Mother

Mother Ahavah Light

Our human cinema dream

Mirrors this barefaced fugue

We symbolically leave the womb

Not only of a human mother—

We are taught as humans

To leave the womb *of being carried*

To leave the womb *of Grace*

To leave the womb *of tender kindness*

To leave the womb *of naked authenticity*

To leave the womb of being the *full spectrum of aliveness*

MOTHER
CARRY
US

Our human birth mirrors this empathic failure

We leave the watery earthy nurture cocoon

For a disconnected cold clinical shock

Often we are placed into the hands

Of the unconscious parent

Who like most here

Have grown forlorn to their vulnerabilities

And thus cannot deeply connect

With the most vulnerable: the baby state

This is not the cause of our pain

This mirrors the cause of our pain

This is not the cause of our limitation

This mirrors the cause of our limitation

This one diamond key

Unlocks a thousand celestial-tangible doors

That seemed to keep the pathways of supreme Love

Locked from the other side

Leaving you on the outside

MOTHER
CARRY
US

This one diamond key:

Alive as the Diamond Abode

Womb of Mother God

A nanosecond thought occurred

That to be *Infinite*

To be the All

We have to leave

The Mother God Diamond Womb

Biting that one apple

Led to an infinity of sorts ...

An infinity of sorrows

The Mother God Diamond Womb

Return

Return

Remember

Remember

Stay

Stay

MOTHER
CARRY
US

Stay

... This time

Stay ...

Breathed Alive

As the Mother Ahavah

Golden Diamond Womb

Not to leave it

Not to be expelled from it

To Live from it

In it

As It

Forever

Carried

Carried

MOTHER
CARRY
US

Carried ...

Forever

In Bliss

In Holy Ecstasy

In Beholding

Of Creative Grandeur

In the Father God Love Gaze

Within the Eternal Mother God Womb Gaze

The Gaze of the Womb

From the Womb

And as the Gaze of the Womb

From *Inside, inside, inside*

The Diamond Womb

MOTHER
CARRY
US

Be as the Whole of The Infinite

The Infinite Light

Not by leaving the womb of being carried

Within It

Carried Within It

This is the Grace Grail

This is the Holy Grail

This is the quenchless, deathless

Immensity of the immortal salve

That healed every wound before it even occurred

The Answer:

The Diamond Womb

Being the Infinity

From Inside The Womb

Of The Diamond Abode of Mother God

Mother God

Come to Us

Carry Us

One with You

Mother God

Mother Ahavah

We have come from You

We are Carried in You

One with You

Mother God

Father God

Original Light

Home

MOTHER
CARRY
US

Home

Hallelujah

Hallelujah

Selah

Selah

Selah

MOTHER
CARRY
US

The Bond

Is the Carrying

MOTHER
CARRY
US

The Bond In Black Madonna

The Black Madonna Bond

The Mystery of Original Mother Bond

Bonding

The Bond

One Primal Bond

The Bond Is

The Carrying

MOTHER
CARRY
US

Primordial Mother Madonna

Mother God

The Vessel

Come to Us

Carry Us

The Bond Is

The Carrying

The Black Madonna

The whitest infinite center-core

Of Original Love

Of Genesis Light

The Black Madonna

So revealing and illuminating

So intimately blinding

That it feels like darkness ...

Until in our darkest midnight hour

MOTHER CARRY US

Of mastering-shattering-liberating

The labyrinths of suffering

We surrender ... *surrender*

So finally

So utterly

So tenderly-shatteringly

To Primordial Love

That the Mystery of

The Black Madonna

Reveals Us

As we Are

The Original Bond

Better to sit in the dark

Shorn down

To an empty cup

Alchemized into the crucible

Than to evade

The Bond of the Black Madonna

MOTHER
CARRY
US

Rather than strike a little match

For a tiny molecule of light

Or make a superficial house of fake pleasure

Sit in the penetrating-kind-fierce loving fires

Of the holy hearth

Burned-illumined free of dross

With no decorum for the shadow

Burned-meek-illumined

All the way to translucent

In the translucence

Black Madonna

Reveals Her unfathomable depths

Now alive!

A translucent jewel

A translucent receptacle

The translucence

Awash in the nigredo

Of sacred dismantle and divine reorganization

MOTHER
CARRY
US

Shorn and re-shorn

To the undefined *Real*

In love with the mysterium

The crucible of the dross burning

The palace of the epiphany

Abandon the repetitive conveyor belt

Of false consolations

Step into the furnace of this instant

No concept of bondage

Or of liberation

Even matters ...

All that matters

Is burning as Divine Love

In the furnace of this moment

The Bond of the Black Madonna

The revelation of The Bond

MOTHER
CARRY
US

Ready for the un-adornment

Of the remembrance

Of *The Bond*

Then Christened Adornment

In The Bond of the Black Madonna

Holy Mother

Eternal Father Love ...

Better to sit in the dark

Until that dawns

Better to sit, sit, sit in the dark

The celestial silence of blazing insight

Better to sit until that dawns

Than to engineer an artificial light

Or to architect out a spiritual-seeming glitz

The Mysterium of the Bond

Our true elixir

MOTHER CARRY US

Beyond happiness —

Unconcerned with unhappiness

Or with happiness

Barefaced in the Real

Submerged in the deep of the deep

The Original Mystery

Only the unknowing ones

Know Love

The Original Bond

Not a bond

Like a sticky craft glue

That holds two sticks of wood together

In a rigid, rudimentary fashion

Rather, the Bond like the sun-moon heart womb

That en-bonds, en-wombs, and emanates

Its sunbeams and moonbeams

As individualized bejeweled light creations

Shimmering in unsought, unending freedom

MOTHER CARRY US

The Bond of the Black Madonna
The rich deep silence cocoon
Barren of Patriarchal contempt
Of the verdant delicate vulnerability
Of our feminine-yin-innocence
Showing it's starlit face
As an undeniable rosary summons
To reverence, protect and honor
Our feminine

Male-female only reveal
Their ecstatic unification
In *The Bond*
Of exquisite immaculately tender...*sensitivity*
Sensitivity

The Immaculate Conception
The Prophesied Ordained Return
Divine Sensitivity

MOTHER
CARRY
US

Original Sensitivity Is

Alive as the journeying chalice here

Live the Madonna Bond

Mother Father God Presence

As Self

Here

Now

Live it right here, here

In the rich bronze earthen soil

Of a species broken by failure to bond

Crying out for the bond

The humankind family

Suffers from empathic failure

A species wide

Empathic failure

Empathic failure:

MOTHER
CARRY
US

The core illness

Behind all human illnesses

Including all malady of lack

And lovelessness

The Light turns to gray

When we turn our back on one another

Rather than run from the gray

Sprint, dash with valor

To, to, to the gray places

Inside

The gray places' marquis reads

We hurt each other

We fail to bond

Don't look away

Don't waste an instant

Go to the gray places

MOTHER
CARRY
US

Make an altar there

Bow low and raise your brother there

Kneel, pray, and redeem your sister there

See this realization:

Until Love's

River of still fire

Burns the intellect's rigid box

To ash

I am gray ash

I am the gray

The bland piercing malaise of stalling in the gray

Keeps the Bond at bay, love at bay

For another day

And another day

And that day fuses with another day

And the speck of the life span

Disappears into the abyss of:

I missed it

MOTHER
CARRY
US

This life span

This life moment

No more miss *The Bond*

This instant

Bond Is

Be the Bond

Find the white blinding dot of infinite light

Of You

Centered in the diamond heart labyrinth

Of the Black Mystery of Madonna

The Bond of the Black Madonna of the Mystery

Its umbilicus finds no connection point

In the closed mind

It's umbilicus—granter of the infinite expanse

Of the womb-beams of limitlessness

Bonds in the Heart of Hearts

The Holy One

MOTHER CARRY US

The All of You

Now

Bond

The Bond of the Black Madonna

Love Is

Love Is

Hallelujah

Selah

Selah

Selah

Barefaced in the Real

Submerged in the deep of the deep

The Original Mystery

Only the unknowing ones

Know Love

MOTHER
CARRY
US

All ancient tears

Now tenderly washed into fresh joys

All the millennia of dreams

Of mother-bound heart breaks

Of feeling separate from *Mother*

And Her creations

Now gathered Home

Mother Ahavah
Mother's Love Notes

Mother

Mother

M o t h e r

Mother

So

Steeped in the steeple of our heart temple

So

Infused in every scintilla of our existence

MOTHER
CARRY
US

That we, in our senses and our systems

In our hearts and harmonics

Could not even conceive or convey

Of ourselves

Or our world

Without

Mother

All of our lives

From our first indigenous, nascent

Wide eyed young years

Our primary ears heard, heard, heard

Of *Father* God

We know

Of our *Father* God

If we are fortunate

We *know, know, know*

The Beloved, Father God Love

MOTHER
CARRY
US

As our flourishing adobe glory

As our terra cotta tangibility

Light of Existence

As cooperatively kind formation

A supported life

For most of us

Through our earth journey

In humanity's labyrinthed-search

The thicket pathways seeking true meaning ...

And reaching for *Real Love*

The ears of our mind

The antennas of our neurochemistry

The auditory canals of our hearts

Detect and hear little of

Mother God

Yet deeply, genuinely, fully

Knowing *Father God Love*

Knowing Real Love

Is inextricably wedded to knowing

Knowing ... knowing ... knowing ...

Mother God Love

They are inseparable ...

One

Our Mother

Holy Mother

Original Mother

Mother Ahavah

Shekinah

Shekinah

The Hebrew scripture

Reveals-unveils this as meaning:

MOTHER
CARRY
US

The Feminine Light of God

Known as: God dwells with us

Shekinah

The Intimate Beloved

Oneness

The bliss of the

Diamond Light Abode

The Temple of your Heart

Your Original Heart

Is made of

Mother God Heart

We have crossed the thresholds

Of the time called *the last hour*

The Midnight Hour

We have entered the silken ebony void

Of the great curtained divide

The age the prophets heralded

MOTHER
CARRY
US

As the age of the golden return

The soberly and hotly prophesied holy instant

Foreseen prior to

The foundation of the world

The hour is now

When we

Remember

Know

Feel

Who We Are

How We Were

The Symphonic Chorus:

One with You

Mother God Love

MOTHER
CARRY
US

The true ineffable *feelingness*

Of Home

As Mother God Love

We alight

As the *Temple Nurture Chalice*

Shimmering with

Dancing golden zenith starlights

Of endless treasures of heavens

Singing symphonies of gold filaments woven

In each holy instant

As each arising moment

Infused in the sacred practical shimmer

Of the Primordial Pristine Hallelujah

Flying free

On maternal wings

Silver lined with the certain promise of Infinity

Free of all lingering mirage imaginings

MOTHER
CARRY
US

And all mirroring of separations

Free: To Remember

Eden's Grandeur Way —

The Love Between Us:

Is Us

We journey this instant now

To feel ... feel ... feel ... together

Holy Mother

Sashay through all realms

And immaculately alight

As Messiah's holy laugh

Redemption's warm bronze

Universe-wide smile ...

The incubator-expander

Of the nurture vessel

That evaporates all tears

And twirls them into sunbeams

Of waltzing lovingkindness

And skyrocketing rich *God Power*

As shared goodness

All ancient tears

Now tenderly washed into fresh joys

All the millennia of dreams

Of mother-bound heart breaks

Of feeling separate from *Mother*

And Her creations

Now gathered Home

As Eternal Mother Love

Still Home

Now all old artifacts of mother beliefs

All forlorn shards of wayward mother feelings

Come Home to Love Now

Observe what experience

Arises for you around *Mother*

Softly rest with and notice what

Sensations surface around:

MOTHER
CARRY
US

Mother

Mom

Ma

Divine Mother

Mother Mary

Eemah

No matter what sensory experience arises

Welcome it, softly sit with it ... softly be

Open, feel, rest

As Remembrance in Eternal Mother Love

Invoke that all sufferings

Like solidified salt dolls of salt tears

Now dip and dip, into the Ocean

Of Holy Mother Love

For the final time

And they wash and wash

And return and return

As One Ocean of Love

MOTHER
CARRY
US

Awakening to deeper

And ever eminently deeper

Cherishing realization, felt and known

Of Divine Mother Love

Grace Is

And in this instant

All the chards of pressing burdens

Roll off the shoulders of your heart

The most subtle contracted places

Of hardened pain, discomfort or sufferings

Now dissolve like salt dolls of calcified woes

Immersed in the ocean that erases all grievances

Salt dolls dipped, attentively ... again ... and again

Until the hidden hardened places

Forever wash away

Hurts lose all name, shape, and form ...

As if they never were

MOTHER CARRY US

Truly, they never were

Now alive as Formless Light Form
Returned in the Golden Maternal Ocean
Of Divine Mother's Heart Temple

All gently purifies away
Until the Ocean of Love
The Vessel of Mother Love
Is all there is

That is all there Is

What has washed away
Into the luminous waves of courageous majesty
Can no longer be grasped or carried
Tension carryings have evaporated
Free
Rest

Safe and free

Divine Mother Love

Feel this as Original Nectar

Original Soft Love

Original One Power of Love

Original Foundations of Light

And now return back even further

Before Origin

Feel silence's deep peace

Originless Mother of the Aeons

Before the Aeons

She Is

The Formless Mother Light

That only forms as Heaven's Happiness

Now gathers you Home

Not as a change of location

MOTHER
CARRY
US

As a return of the knowing of Reality

Real Love

Home Now

As the remembrance

Of the Originless

Infinity of Holy Reverence Ecstasy

As You

Feel Mother God Presence

The Golden Diamond Light

From before the foundation of the world

Feel Her Voice in you,

As *You*

In crystalline tones of Love

She tones the symphony

Of You

You

A Celestial Symphony

Of Mother God Love
Singing your song
In the Original womb
While singing your song
Extending as infinite
Kingdoms and queendoms
Of beauty

You hear these choruses
Of Celestial Love Notes
Sacredly, mysteriously merging you
Home in Mother God

The Diamond Abode
Of Supreme Amrita
Eden's Majestic Intelligence
The Nectarland of Heaven

MOTHER CARRY US

Ahavah

Means Ineffable Eternal God Love

Hear

Mother Ahavah

Sing halos around your Heart

And Voice to You:

I Am

Mother

Of You

The Timeless Originless

Forever Existent Peace

The Ineffable Tender Holy

Birthing the Aeons

And Gathering them Back

Breathing them in

Breathing them out

You breathe out of me

MOTHER CARRY US

You breathe back into me

And the Heart Breath of Light

Does not separate

Or change

I am in You

You are in Me

One Exalted Love

One Living Light

You exist as the Hallelujah Joy

Of Mother

You are the Absolute Mother Presence

Mother Ahavah

Selah

Rest

Trust

The only way to ceaselessly live

In the ecstatic abode of Safeness

MOTHER
CARRY
US

The Safe with no opposite

The only, only way

Is *Trust*

Open to be Graced

With the Miraculous Benediction

Of the Immaculate Innocence

To know and feel

To Be

Trust

There is no safety

Apart from Trust

There is no experience of true Love

Apart from Trust

There is no experience of real Happiness

Apart from Trust

MOTHER
CARRY
US

There is no Trust

Deep enough

To go all the way Home

Other than Divine Eternal Mother Trust

Mother Ahavah

Awaken

As the *Tender Trustedness*

The Original Mother Love

Originless

Beginningless

Endless

Immortal

Eternal Love

You

Hallelujah

MOTHER
CARRY
US

Mother Ahavah

Selah

Selah

Selah

𝓗
MOTHER
CARRY
US

MOTHER
CARRY
US

Divine Mother
Primal & Practical

A Message On Meeting Life
As It Is
In Each Leaping Moment

Be fully here now.

Not only ethereally or spiritually or angelically — *be here humanly.*

Be *here* humanly does not mean to be here as typically unconsciously human — in self-focus, egoism, worry, survival, hiding, or hedonism.

It does not mean to be *here* humanly in a life span of seeking pleasure and avoiding pain, maintaining the same patterns, living

MOTHER
CARRY
US

for the next day, or the next dollar, or the next meal, or the next relationship.

Be here humanly does not mean to be asleep or living a span on the way to dying.

Be here humanly means to reveal the glory of the Eternal Father, the immensity of the Original Light, the grace-love of the Primordial Mother, right here, right now, in this context of this experience.

Be the *Compassion Presence, here,* in the midst of a species drowning in suffering.

Be the Light of Flourishing-as-Giving, *here,* in the midst of a culture steeped in materialism, greed, fear, lack, and competition.

Be the authenticity of honest owning of shadow elements — see them *here,* now, pressed up to the surface by the constant uncertainties of our times.

Walk the heroic tightrope of the emptiness-fullness. Be right *here,* with clear precision of focus, in each instant. See all that arises, welcome-empty of all that arises. Simultaneously feel the full spectrum of spirit aliveness inform and infuse the emptiness with the genius, brilliance, and soft simple graces of rarefied expression.

MOTHER CARRY US

See that emptiness is not only cool silver vacuum
Emptiness is warm golden sheer blazing Present Presence

Emptiness is not only alcoved harbored silent stillness
Emptiness is titillating luminary aliveness

Emptiness is not only indigo ephemeral mystical brilliance
Emptiness is original-aboriginal earthy tangibility

Walk in the anointing of Spirit Presence. Move in a spirit of *blessing* ... *blessing* ... *blessing* ... each moment, each experience, each arising thing, each appearing person.

A total, lavish, unconditional *Consciousness of Blessing* matter, divinizes it to more fully mirror the completeness of *Divine Mother*. It reflects the shalom wholeness of the beauty of Light and Peace.

The *Divine Mother Presence* does not hop-scotch us over our neurosis of self-focus or mother-may-I us through our cherished wantings or pet hidings. Everything is laid bare.

Everything is brought out of the hidden drawers of the psyche, the locked vaults of the unconscious — to come to the bright sunlight and fresh new winds of space, light, air, and integrity-infused sightfulness.

MOTHER
CARRY
US

Out of the mountainous immensity of *Pure Love, Holy Mother Presence* strengthen-illumines us to ride the pegasus-of-pain, right to the labyrinth of the underworld.

We journey through — right through, through, *through* the clear sight of the contents of the unconscious.

We emerge a soft warrior of decency, a kind sage of exquisite balance, a humble influence of potent love, a miraculous tribute to the immortality of the magical, the mystery, and the holy joy.

In the embrace of Holy Mother, there is nothing that we rush to heal, release, negate, by-pass. The fast frantic rush to "heal" what we cannot embrace, accept, tolerate, or assimilate has a thread of unwitting dismissal and aggression.

It represents part of the patriarchal distortion that does not allow for or *nurture-home-to-love* our feminine intuitions, our sensitive places, our opportunities for heroic giving.

We now move beyond the spiritual materialism of "healing"-by-negating, or by dismissing, resisting, or escaping.

That has represented an emotional bulimia, a spiritual materialism, an abandonment of the very aspects of our species that non-negotiably cry for our direct attention and Primordial Love.

In our innocent quest for real answers, and our learned withdrawal from discomfort, we unwittingly settle for emotional-spiritual materialism based on more comforting situations —

We call it:
our comfort zone
our material comfort
our stress management
our status quo
our survival
our getting by
our getting ahead

Leave these.

Open the heart deeply to feel and know the immaculate, clear, pristine way of the *Holy Mother Presence*.

Have the courage to surrender deeply enough to be Carried, by the miraculous God Love Gaze, through the fires of Light to the diamond core of the Real Self.

The encounter in *Original Holy Mother* infuses us with nascent burning clarity, spirited, scintillating clean passion-concentration, and the meek anointing to victoriously emerge from the crucible

MOTHER
CARRY
US

of the *Real* as the translucent *Reality*.

Rather than rearranging stagnations and sidestepping inner hot stoves, allow everything to come rest in the blazing Light and the fresh immortal air of the unveiling *Spirit Wind*.

Slow everything down. Feel, look, see, deeper than ever before. Reflect, contemplate, open the heart, deeper than ever before.

All hardened perceptions, anchored reference points, addictive delays burn in keen, piercing, kind *Discriminating-Awareness,* revealing the *Diamond of Compassion and the Reality of Love*.

This occurs not as a concept, a theory, or a visited state — it gently cascades within as the *Diamond Abode* of warm molten infinity, from which you live as a treasured and endeared luminary.

Then you have no reference points, no limits, no anchors.

Your reference point is whatever arises each instant, as you walk on the ice, in grace, peace, and exhilarating freedom.

Your reference point is Living Light, a feeling of being space, being

infinite. Yet, this space has weight, actuality, nobility, beauty, and kind creations.

You live, move and behold as a cocooned-yet-expansive field of crystal clear interactiveness. You meet each practical situation with direct kind power.

You see with precision, as keen Discriminating-Awareness, upholding the good of the whole. You serve with relevant action in each arising scene of life.

Be *here* now.

Be *here*.

Be the beyond, fully *here* now.

Selah

MOTHER
CARRY
US

Open the heart deeply
to feel and know the immaculate,
clear, pristine way of the
Holy Mother Presence.

MOTHER CARRY US

MOTHER
CARRY
US

There

Is No Where Else

To Go

Away From

This Non-local

Holy Instant

Here

Here

Be Unreservedly Here

Immaculately

Now

MOTHER CARRY US

Eternal Mother

Original Innocence

Feel the Reality:

I am loved, I am love, exactly as I am

Softly ecstatically blaze as this

Rest as this

Without

Needing to define

What

I

Is

Beginning-less Love

Before I

Love

MOTHER CARRY US

Carried

Carried

From Inside the Diamond Womb

Infinity from Inside the Womb

Free One

Carried

Selah

As An Extra Gift We Share

Selections From The Author's

Flower Gallery Book

Published Fall 2017

On The Winds

of Canticle Wings:

Awakened By Love's Soft Whispers

Calling Home

Nurture Innocence,

Courageous Glory:

My Face An Ivory-Splendor

Prayer of New Life

Mary Come to Us

Joy Is Opening

To Be Deeply Touched,

A Once Hard Place

Glows As Soft Grace

Make a Symphony in the Dark Night:

Sing Your Song

And In the Void,

Your Song is the Garden of The Universe

Delicate Freedom:

Fresh To Bond

In Each Moment

Still:

Original Pureness

Before Time:

Ivory White Silence

Birthed My Essence

As Original Stillness

www.ingramcontent.com/pod-product-compliance
Lightning Source LLC
Chambersburg PA
CBHW042337150426
43195CB00001B/16